Warwic

ies

, Jorking, for

Warw
Count

D1420298

013974585 X

ALL ONE BREATH

BY THE SAME AUTHOR

FICTION
The Dumb House
The Mercy Boys
Burning Elvis
The Locust Room
Living Nowhere
The Devil's Footprints
Glister
A Summer of Drowning
Something Like Happy

POETRY
The Hoop
Common Knowledge
Feast Days
The Myth of the Twin
Swimming in the Flood
A Normal Skin
The Asylum Dance
The Light Trap
The Good Neighbour
Selected Poems
Gift Songs
The Hunt in the Forest
Black Cat Bone

NON-FICTION
A Lie About My Father
Waking Up in Toytown

ALL ONE BREATH

John Burnside

CAPE POETRY

Published by Jonathan Cape 2014

2 4 6 8 10 9 7 5 3 1

Copyright © John Burnside 2014

John Burnside has asserted his right under the Copyright, Designs
and Patents Act 1988 to be identified as the author of this work

This book is sold subject to the condition that it shall not,
by way of trade or otherwise, be lent, resold, hired out,
or otherwise circulated without the publisher's prior
consent in any form of binding or cover other than that
in which it is published and without a similar condition,
including this condition, being imposed
on the subsequent purchaser

First published in Great Britain in 2014 by
Jonathan Cape
Random House, 20 Vauxhall Bridge Road,
London SW1V 2SA

www.randomhouse.co.uk

Addresses for companies within The Random House Group Limited can be found at:
www.randomhouse.co.uk/offices.htm

The Random House Group Limited Reg. No. 954009

A CIP catalogue record for this book is available from the British Library

ISBN 9780224097406

The Random House Group Limited supports the Forest Stewardship Council® (FSC®),
the leading international forest-certification organisation. Our books carrying the FSC
label are printed on FSC®-certified paper. FSC is the only forest-certification
scheme supported by the leading environmental organisations, including Greenpeace.
Our paper procurement policy can be found at www.randomhouse.co.uk/environment

Typeset in Bembo by Palimpsest Book Production Limited,
Falkirk, Stirlingshire

Printed and bound in Great Britain by
CPI Group (UK) Ltd, Croydon CR0 4YY

for Louise

For that which befalleth the sons of men befalleth beasts;
even one thing befalleth them: as the one dieth, so dieth the other;
yea, they have all one breath; so that a man hath no preeminence
above a beast

Ecclesiastes

Mark how one string, sweet husband to another,
Strikes each in each by mutual ordering,
Resembling sire and child and happy mother
Who, all in one, one pleasing note do sing:
  Whose speechless song, being many, seeming one,
  Sings this to thee: 'Thou single wilt prove none.'

William Shakespeare

CONTENTS

NATURAL HISTORY   57

Self Portrait as Funhouse Mirror

We can be redeemed only to the extent to which we see ourselves.

Martin Buber

I HALL OF MIRRORS, 1964

Quam angusta innocentia est,
ad legem bonum esse.
                              Seneca

It wasn't a fairground so much;
just an acre of clay on old man Potter's land
where someone had set up shop
to amuse the locals,

mayweed and trampled grass beneath our feet,
the perfumes that passed for summer
in towns like ours
touched, now, with the smell of candy floss

and diesel, and the early evening dusk
made eerie by those strings of *famille-verte*
and powdered-citrus light-bulbs round the stalls
where goldfish in their hundreds probed the walls

of fishtanks for the missing scent
of river.
That day, my mother wore her rose-print
sundress, antique-green

and crimson in the off-white
fabric, some new flora growing wild
in infinite reflection, while I turned
and turned, and couldn't find myself until

she picked me out: a squat
intruder in the garden she had made,
blearfaced and discontent, more beast than boy,
more fiend than beast.

That wasn't me, of course; I knew as much;
and yet I knew the creature I had seen
and, when I turned again and saw him
gazing back at me, *ad infinitum*,

I knew him better: baby-faced
pariah; little
criminal, with nothing to confess
but narrow innocence

and bad intentions.
The backrooms of the heart are Babylon
incarnate, miles of verdigris and tallow and the cries
of hunting birds, unhooded for a kill

that never comes.
I saw that, when I saw this otherself
suspended in its caul of tortured glass,
and while I tried pretending not to see, my mind

a held breath in a house I'd got by heart
from being good according to a law
I couldn't comprehend, I saw
– and I believed my mother saw –

if only for a moment, what I was
beyond the child she loved, the male
homunculus she'd hoped I'd never find
to make me like my father, lost

and hungry, and another mouth to feed
that never quit its ravening.
A moment passed;
I was convinced she'd seen,

but when I turned to look, her face was all
reflection, printed roses and a blear
of Eden from that distance in the glass,
where anything can blossom, Judas tree and tree

of knowledge, serpents gnawing at the roots, the life
perpetual, that's never ours alone,
including us, till everything
is choir.

II SELF PORTRAIT

The one thing you want to portray
is the one thing it lacks.

Awareness, perhaps, the sense of an outside world:
a holly tree, starlings, the neighbour who plays piano,

or somebody out on the staircase, pausing to listen
for longer than you had expected.

You do this again and again, as if your life
depended on nothing,

light filtered up from the alley, the homeward sound
of shoppers and that constant sense you have

of some place less than half a mile from here,
a favourite bar, a pool hall, someone's bed,

the place you could be right now, with snow coming down
through neon, or that baize light on your hands

that makes you think of summers long ago,
the 'water's edge', the 'faint breeze in the pines',

those girls you really loved, before this patient
look-alike paid forfeit to the dark.

III MY GRANDMOTHER'S HOUSE

en el espejo pinta
un paisaje más dulce que el paisaje,
un adiós más eterno que el del día
                          Juan Ramón Jiménez

After she hung that mirror in the hall
the world was changed forever.
It wasn't just reveal; there was a far
white distance at the corner of the glass,
a thousand miles of tundra, just beyond
the climbing roses twined around her door.

Whenever we went to visit, I was the one
who ventured out over the snow, in a havering wind,
to name the flora there, my only point
of reference a childhood I had lost
on purpose, and such Bible litanies
as anyone remembers;

nothing but stunted willows, clumps of birch,
a scatter of Arctic
poppies, miniature
as any signal is, Druidic greens
and greys I'd only learn to recognise
by being lost.

If only the body offered such
taxonomies: a name for every shade
of fever, or those dark interiors
where snow has passed beyond
the picturesque, those first flakes in the dusk
become a months–long standstill, shapes and sounds

that made me think
of furnace, every scent
a symptom, sweet
urea in the creases of my palms,
cloves at the back of my throat
like a cherished tumour.

After she died, I watched my favourite uncle
lower the glass from the wall and set it down
so all it could reflect was polished wood
and lino, though the soul it had beguiled
kept walking into blizzard, dumb to grief,
and nothing he could track to bring him home.

IV POWER CUT WITH CHEVAL MIRROR (HOMAGE TO THOMAS HARDY)

for my sons

You woke up in the dark and came
to find me,

a sickle moon shedding its light
in the narrow hall,

that give in the floorboards
footworn and hollowed

and thin
              – but you weren't afraid so much
as confused: the doorwells

occupied, all of a sudden,
by something new,

the feel of the house unfamiliar, its fabric
wedded to the land

around us, seeing eyes where we
were blind.

Yet isn't there a hint of *Thou* to find
in how the light reveals us all as wisps

of distance in the mirror, when the candle
wavers for a moment and we're lost

in depth of field, a newfound history
of presence in the dark, its self-unseeing

barely the ghost you feared
or hoped for; just

the long familiar things
made strange, as if you'd turned to find

your bearings
                    – home
as love and narrative –

while, just this once,
the known world looked away.

V THE WAKE

In a house with too many mirrors,
it's hard to dream;
and this is why, after she died,
her children walked the house from room to room,
with sheets and scarves to blind each looking glass
that might have kept her from the afterlife.

No one explained; and yet I understood
how readily the soul might linger on –
a far song in the hollow of the roof,
a thumbprint on a cup, an old cologne.

A mercy, then, to send them out alone,
forgetting what they were, no name, no face:
whatever happens in the life to come,
you'd hardly want to drag the self along.

My uncles left that house of mirrors wrapped
for weeks, a secret flowering on the glass
beneath the veils of blanket-wool and linen;
and, afterwards, I couldn't bear to look,
afraid that I might catch her hurrying back
to what she'd always known, an eager ghost,
smiling at nothing, coming home untransformed.

VI A RIVAL

Sometimes, when I watch you through the glass,
fixing your make-up, or twisting your hair in a plait,
I catch a passing glimpse of someone new,
someone I might have loved had we ever met
and, now that we've come this far, I must admit
that, given the choice, I'd rather her than you:
this inward self a camera might steal,
the soul that shatters when a mirror breaks
and, so they say, takes seven years to heal.
Sometimes I think if she and I were free,
she'd tell me secrets you could never share;
though, now I come to think of it, I swear
I've caught her giving you such private looks
as lovers do, when no one else can see
and then I've turned away, for all our sakes,
because it's clear she'd rather you than me.

VII SELF PORTRAIT AS
PICTURE WINDOW

First day of snow, the low sun
glinting on the gate post where a single
Teviot ewe is licking
frost-melt from the bars, the other sheep
away in the lower field, the light on the crusted
meadow grass that makes me think
of unripe plums so local an event
it seems, for one long breath,
that time might stop;
or, better, that it isn't me at all
who stands here, at this window, gazing out,
not me who woke up late, when everyone
had gone to work or school, but someone else,
a man so like myself that nobody
would spot the difference – same eyes, same mouth –
but gifted with a knowledge I can scarcely
register in words, unless I call it
graceful and nomadic, some lost art
of finding home in sheep trails, lines of flight,
the feel of distance singing in the flesh
and happiness-as-forage, bedding in,
declining, making sense of what it finds.

VIII A COUPLE

And is this your heart arithmetic?
    Carl Sandburg

Some nights I wake and find you in the dark,
your face too close, a blur of sweat and hair,
the inadvertent cling of heat and skin
against my throat or shoulder.

It takes some time to turn you, like a child,
shifting your weight, then edging you aside
till something in you gives and you roll over,
the exercise matter-of-fact, emotionless:

careful neglect, a practised, *unheimlich* manoeuvre.
Some nights I sit up late, afraid to sleep,
because of what I'd tell, if I should dream.
Such secrets as I have, I pray to keep.

Yet though I see myself for what I am,
I've never thought the heart was rag and bone,
only a looking glass where slow decay
allows the darkness in through broken silver;

so when you catch me looking through the mirror
at someone other than the self you are,
pretend, for pity's sake, that you're alone
as I have done for years, in borrowed rooms

with other bodies, waking with a start
to sweat and hair, a cling of heat and skin
I barely know until I struggle free
and lie apart again, remembering you

as once I thought you, when I thought you true.

IX A NEW ANATOMY

It must be age, I think,
when I look back and see those snaps
from my mother's album,

that seven- or eight-year-old, who would have become
an expert on fog or the genus
Sterna, had he been able,

sealed in the shadowy glint
of a funhouse mirror
and grinning at the only living soul

he loves for sure.
It must be a kind of weathering, not to regret
the life he's lived: the histories of smog

and birdsong, lost; the long
subjunctive of the missed and overlooked,
lost in the local theatre of self-

as-prodigal, the apple of her eye
playing for laughs, a straw-patterned KISS ME QUICK hat
perched (rakishly, he thinks)

on his crew-cut skull.
There's something in her steadiness he sees
as holy, like a chapel in the woods

— the green of it, a constant putting up
of appleseed and honey in the sight
of heaven, that unseemly everafter —

but now, as he stands leering through the glass,
it scares him, till he longs to disappear,
somebody's changeling, cherished but not what was wanted,

compelled to forage, hungry,
undesired —

A room inside a room, all light and air
until we enter through a mirrored door
that, when we close it, folds into the wall
and disappears.
It's almost empty; light above our heads
then space beneath us, so it seems we'll fall –
father and son, gone gently to the dark
like Alice, in her slow-mo rabbit hole.
He tells me it's a *Spiegelkabinett*
– he read it on a sign, but doesn't know
what that would be in English.
I think a while, then say: *A Mirror Maze,*
remembering that scene where Orson Welles
and Rita Hayworth – recently divorced –
kill their reflections over and over again
in *Lady from Shanghai.*
He's making random faces in the glass
to test himself, mock variants of loss
and cartoon fear, mad genius, evil twin;
he works them out, then calls so I can look
– no point pretending, if it isn't shared –
and though I'm smiling, what I think he sees
is worry and cause for worry, how my life
is not the life he thinks of, when he thinks
of being happy.
I want to say *it's fine, it's just not
how you think it is, or ought to be* –
but now I'm at the centre of the room
turning around to see myself again
and then again, arrested in the glass,
an Everyman with nothing in his face
but fifty years of average wear and tear,
and somewhere, in those halted satyr's eyes,
a stray voice from the schoolyard, folded neat

and put away a lifetime for safekeeping.
It's me, of course, and yet, if I were pressed,
I couldn't say who that man's father is,
and no one here could be my father's son;
what's father to this shadow of a man
is some bright flaw or phantom in the child
he played for years, a glimmering of wild
that never showed itself, except in passing;
what's son to him, a child he can't protect
from public cheats and smug self-regulation,
liars in boardrooms, neighbours he cannot trust,
and children making sport of what he hopes
will last; because they do: we're always
fearful of the image in the glass
that might, in some far nightmare, find us out
as mine does: me, my father, no man's son,
the stumbling figure in the mirror maze
who knows what's right – he's talking about love –
but cannot make it happen, though the shots
ring out and all those persons he became
are shattered, till there's nothing but the frame
where no one stands, though almost anyone
could find his way, through love and loss of love,
to this finale, orphaned, far for home.

Devotio Moderna

AT THE ENTERING OF THE NEW YEAR
(HOMAGE TO THOMAS HARDY)

The future isn't what it used to be
Yogi Berra

Since it's not what it used to be,
the future is ours,

years to regret the bodies we dissolved
in Pinot Noir

and Paracetamol,
a decade or more to walk home in the rain

repeatedly, the yard light coming on
as if by magic;

and, having come this far,
can we take it as read

that nothing ever happens
for a reason,

that choosing is out of the question, as is luck,
and the surest mistake

is to think we already know
what matters when we see it?

A week of fog;
a strange car in the driveway;

a doll's house
in a front yard,

pearled with rain —
no one can read the signs, it's not

a narrative;
if moths know anything of love

it has nothing to do with the beautiful doom
we long for;

and if what we insist on calling
fate seems inexplicable or cruel

it's only because
we lack the imagination

to wish for what it brings,
to brighten it

with something more inventive
than dismay.

Late in the day,
but we're starting to like ourselves

and something feels true
that was always

in doubt
when it counted,

not what we know, but the things
we've decided to keep,

a ribbon of wilderness
out on the rim of our days,

the fine-grain of happy, the snowstorms,
the art of fugue,

some thirteen-minute loop
of grainy footage

running, for auld lang's syne,
at the back of our minds.

RETURN OF THE PRODIGAL SON

after Sebald Beham, 1538

Bad luck for the calf.
Head back, it lies
on the butcher's table, heart and liver
spooned into a bowl, a pail
of blood and innards
waiting to be drained
and given to the dogs.
The other son looks on.
He's been rebuked, but then
he's used to that.
Besides, he's the reasoning kind,
a man who's seen enough of life to know
that change is not
so easy, few
can mend their ways,
once they've acquired a taste
for elsewhere.
Meanwhile, the father goes
from room to room,
greeting his friends and neighbours, all those guests
who pitied him for years, cut down to size
by something that will feel
like triumph, if he works it hard enough.
He's hired musicians
– boys with flutes and harps –
enough noise, and he might convince himself
that this is all he needs: the greying wife
consoled for years of grief,
the child he once thought lost
come back to life
and bound to him
by duty

and repentance.
Out in the yard
the dogs have abandoned the pail;
tipped over on its side, it oozes
blood clots and threads of bile, the moonlight
pooling on a spill
of fat and matter;
yet someone on the high road, passing through
and hearing music at the open door,
would think it was a birthday, or a wedding,
the tallowed gold of home, ringed round with vines,
a single lantern
in the attic window.

JOSEPH WRIGHT OF DERBY:
AN EXPERIMENT ON A BIRD IN THE AIR PUMP, 1768

He travels from town to town
with his apparatus;
a showman with wild white hair and incurious eyes,
he brings a touch of theatre to the lives
of squires and merchants, boys in love with death
and troubled girls who know this world is cruel
for reasons of their own.
Wherever he peddles his trade,
it's always the same,
air pump and glass receiver, *memento mori,*
the flutter in the bowl just one more
instance of casual slaughter (tonight's cockatoo
a rare and theatrical
flourish: more often he uses
some common or garden bird,
say a lark, or a sparrow).
While one hand works the pump, the other
hangs above the cover as the subject
struggles to stay alive,
a note of panic brightening the room
until the creature fades and what remains
is empty matter.
Lately, they're all the rage,
these Pneumatical Engines,
amateurs build them at home, playing god for an hour,
owls in the deer park, a smatter of rain at the window,
the ticking of the clock, by which to time
the game of life and death:
I killed in the vacuum many
Animals that breath, as Birds, Mice, Rats,
Rabbets,
Cats;

some of them I recovered
by quickly giving them Air before
the Engine was quite exhausted;
but I never saw any revive,
that had been in a perfect vacuum.
One girl stares in fascinated
horror at the dying cockatoo;
another girl covers her eyes, while her father
points as if to say that grace will come
when the showman opens the vent – though grace delayed
is ever its own reward and, besides,
that well-dressed man in the foreground
is utterly rapt,
as is the boy
who might be his son and heir, their immaculate faces
half in the rouge-coloured shadows, their arms
akimbo, it seems, as they wait for the end to come:
but notwithstanding this hurt, the Lark
was very lively,
and did divers times spring up
to a good height.
The Vessel being hastily, but carefully closed,
the Pump was diligently plyed,
and the Bird for a while appeared lively enough;
but upon a greater Exsuction of the Air,
she began manifestly to droop
and appear sick,
and very soon after was taken
with as violent and irregular convulsions,
as are wont to be observed
in Poultry, when their heads are wrung off:
For the Bird threw her self over and over
two or three times,
and dyed with her Breast upward,
her Head downwards,
and her Neck awry.

The moon is full tonight, though we barely see it
up in the topmost corner, a sliver of cloud
bisecting it neatly, though nobody here can know
the world it illumines, the fox cubs crossing the lawn,
the owl floating out from the quincunx of elms in the park
and the silence that follows a kill, when everything stops,
that held breath over the land
till the dead move on.

DEVOTIO MODERNA

But love always moves each man according to the profit and the ability of each.

John of Ruysbroeck

This is the life: a pause for the briefest
rehearsal of someone else
at the back of my mind,

the soul friend
as the hollow of a bowl,
or how the house would smell
if I were gone.

It comes across as something
ancient, stark
caesura and the light that signs me out
from everything I know about the world,

the light of what could seem abandonment,
its weight and fit
like folkright, or good favour;

though, really, it's nothing more than one last
courtesy imposed by *ding an sich,*
now that I've come to the end
of my picture book world,

hand-coloured field guides and several different
species of oriole, lost in the turn of a page,
foxgloves and that childhood

pink that doesn't happen any more,
towpaths, a sense of occasion, rotation farming,
unspoken love, the seasons, alpenglow.

Some bitterness, perhaps; but, truth to tell,
I could be fond of anything right now
as long as it came from a place
that didn't feel interrupted,

no question of what we mean when we say
familiar,
the print of sand or heathland on the skin

or how I have tried, in passing, to describe
the quiet, when a last train pulls away
and leaves me on the platform, something bright
and watchful at the far end of the tracks,

a ghost, of sorts, though no one I would know,
much like the sound a neighbour makes, coming downstairs
on New Year's morning, silence on the streets

and every window
strung with coloured lights,
crimson and gold,
to tell the lives of others.

THE END

He who remembers, forgets.
Chinese saying

Strangers are making love
in my grandmother's house
forty years after she died
on a midsummer's morning.
I like to think of them
as happy, more or less;
but sometimes the man
is restless and, after a while,
he gets out of bed
and wanders from room to room,
touching his lover's things, her cloisonné
ring trees
and amberglass jars.
If I could, I would tell him
a story I heard long ago
from a woman with ash-coloured hair
in plum-blossom time.
It's a story he doesn't know,
but halfway through
he sees that it has to end
in the safety of fog,
a black tree laden with fruit
when the first light breaks
on the walls of the dowager's
palace, the ash on the hearthstone
pink with remembered flames
from an empire ago.
I like to think this end will make him
happy, after a fashion;
happiness being the knowledge
that someone is safe

and ready to walk again
in the mothering world:
the boy in the forest,
safe, and the princess-infanta
safe, while my grandmother sleeps
for decades, her body adrift
in acres of blossom
and rain, a silvered
variant of waking that resembles
nothing so much
as that morning, far in the past,
when she stood for a moment
waiting, before she forgot
the who and the where,
a last frost burning away
the night-time shapes of twisted
plum trees
and the empty branches strung
with skin and stones
like tender nubs
of canker.

OFFICIUM

If therefore thou shalt not watch, I will come on thee as a thief,
and thou shalt not know what hour I will come upon thee.

Revelation 3:3

It comes to us, after a time,
that there's no forever:

chiffchaff in the hedge, a breath of wind,
that wave of longing in the summer grass

for something other
than the world we've seen;

and how we've waited years for an event
that couldn't happen:

footprints in the dew
and *adsit nobis*

sudden in our hearts
like summer rain.

Spiritus Sancti: crickets, thistledown,
a wave of longing in the blood-lit dark

for what we are
beyond the things we seem;

and quiet, like the ceasing of a drum,
this penitence by halves is scant relief,

if somewhere in the house, unheard, unseen,
eternity comes creeping, like a thief.

Life Class

HÔTEL DE GRAVE

Nunc, et in hora mortis nostrae

Sometimes I am troubled by the light
that streams across the wall, then disappears,

since every car that passes might be yours:
you at the wheel, your body full of night

– cicada songs, the scent of marguerites,
the minor key of grace that runs for hours

on country roads, beneath a tide of stars
more felt than seen. I'm sluggish with the heat

and far too ready, these days, to believe
you're there – a resurrection, driving south

for hours, *in hora mortis*, to arrive
intact, beneath my window: time of death

a fiction, in the oleander dawn,
and footprints, new as rain, crossing the lawn.

AT MY FATHER'S FUNERAL

The idea that the body as well as the soul was immortal was probably linked on to a very primitive belief regarding the dead, and one shared by many peoples, that they lived on in the grave. This conception was never forgotten, even in regions where the theory of a distant land of the dead was evolved, or where the body was consumed by fire before burial. It appears from such practices as binding the dead with cords, or laying heavy stones or a mound of earth on the grave, probably to prevent their egress, or feeding the dead with sacrificial food at the grave, or from the belief that the dead come forth not as spirits, but in the body from the grave.

J. A. MacCulloch, *The Religion of the Ancient Celts*

We wanted to seal his mouth
with a handful of clay,
to cover his eyes
with the ash of the last

bonfire he made
at the rainiest edge
of the garden

and didn't we think, for a moment,
of crushing his feet
so he couldn't return to the house
at Halloween

to stand at the window,
smoking and peering in,
the look on his face

like that flaw in the sway of the world
where mastery fails

and a hinge in the mind
swings open – grief

or terror coming loose
and drifting, like a leaf,
into the fire.

TOD UND VERKLÄRUNG

My father comes back from the dead,
having been transfigured.
Now, he's a tracker, out on the edge of the town,
following a line of cloven prints
to where the snow begins, beyond the pines.
He's slower now, and careful of the world
around him, so there's space enough for me
to follow after, nothing to betray
or harbour, in the knotwork of the heart,
and barely a glimmer to show
for the fallow deer
that frays against the wind till it steps free,
no backward glance, no scent, no mere redemption,
only a gap in the snow, when it slips away.

THE DAY ETTA DIED

I was marking a stack of essays
on Frank O'Hara

and each had a Wiki-
paragraph to say

who Genet was, and who
was Billie Holiday

– just as this poem stumbles to its end, predictably
remembering the cold December night

I slow-danced with Annabelle Gray to 'I'd Rather Go Blind'
at the Catholic Club Xmas Party,

trees lit with frost outside and cherry-coloured
streetlamps round the playground at Our Lady's,

and here and there, on windows dark with soot
our blurred reflections, sightless in the glass

yet guiding each other, soundlessly, into the sway
of the future, almost swooning from the close

proximity of skin
and muddled breathing.

ALL YOU NEED

The feeling he thinks of as love
is liking the sound of her voice

or how she considers laughing
before she smiles,

and though the words he speaks are learned
from radio and 50s musicals

he isn't that far wrong in thinking
love is like the story he has longed

for years to tell, on such a night as this,
clumsy, no doubt, his fingers

tangled in her shirt, her kiss
so close it feels like someplace in his mind

he hasn't found till now, a borderland
of rain and firs, some distance from the town

he never quite grew up in, lacking her:
and so he says it, loyal to events

he knows enough to trust – this film, that song –
love you he says, though now it seems for show,

a line that runs so far from what he meant,
it frightens him that thinking made it so.

MY GRANDMOTHER, ELIZABETH
BURNSIDE, 1962

Before she could die at home where she belonged,
they took her to St Margaret's hospital
and put her in a room above the town,
first snow at the glass, the buses
heading out to Crossgates and Lumphinnans,
those silver lights below me, where I peered
from breath-fogged windows in the corridor,
waiting to take my turn, three walls away
and her in the high bed, under a plain white sheet,
yellowed and cold, while her grandchildren came, one by one,
to say their goodbyes.
I remember my uncle David leading me in
to kiss her, the skin of her face
dry as old beech leaves, the smell of her sweet and dark
through the lavender talc.
Seven years old, I thought I would see her again,
though I knew she was dying,
for this was a ritual, emotional legalese,
like refusing the last slice of cake, or writing
thank you cards.
For as long as I'd lived,
I had gone to her house once a month
with my mother and sister
to sit by the fire, drinking squash,
her smiling as if it were funny, when she told
how her father had walked all the way
from Ennis to Dublin,
children in tow, her mother always
pregnant, or so it seemed,
then northwards by boat and train, through a rumour
of heathland and loch, a rumour that passed in the dark
till they set down at Cowdenbeath,
sectarian, ugly, and no reason not to move on

beyond fatigue.

But that was our home, she said, by which she meant
that the harder it is to begin with, the prouder we are
to a call a place our own, as she had done
by making a garden of sorts from the pit town's
clinker and soot, her flowerbeds
thick with bees, the housefront
covered with climbing roses, a may hedge
screening it all from the road, and a constant
riot of sparrows, safe from the neighbours' cats,
all squabble and jeer
in the scribbles of shadow and thorn.
What she loved most, I think,
was variegation,
hairstreak, the broken line, the not quite
finished of the moments as they tumbled
one into the next
and never stopped.
Nothing defined, the world
all guesswork: birds,
then shadows, cold rain
spooling through the porch light when she went
to fetch the coal.
I think back and now it's gone, the rumour of heathland
sold to the lowest bidder, the rain
commoditised, a thousand tribes of bees
lost in the haze
of neonicotine.
I kissed her and said goodbye – I'm saying it still –
not quite convinced that anyone can cease
and as I turn to go
her face is lit
from somewhere I can't make out, not the lamp in the room
or the lights from the buses below, as they make their way
to Perth and Glenrothes, Kirkcaldy,
the Bow of Fife.

ON THE VANISHING OF MY SISTER,
AGED 3, 1965

They saw her last in our garden of stones and willows.
A few bright twigs and pebbles glazed with rain
and, here and there, amidst the dirt and gravel,
a slick of leaf and milkstone, beautiful
for one long moment in the changing light.
Then she was gone.
My mother had looked away
for a matter of seconds
– she said this, over and over,
as if its logic could undo
the wildness of a universe that stayed
predictable for years, then carried off
a youngest daughter;
my father was in the room at the back of our prefab,
watching the new TV, the announcer
excited, Gold Cup Day
and Arkle romping home by twenty lengths.
Maybe we have to look back, to see
that we have all the makings of bliss – the first spring light,
the trees along the farm road
thick with song;
and surely it was this
that drew her out
to walk into the big
wide world, astonished, suddenly at home
no matter where she was.
It seems, when they found her,
she wasn't the least bit scared.
An hour passed, then another;
my mother waited, while our friends and neighbours
came and went, my father running out
to search, then back again,
taking her, once, in his arms, and trying

vainly to reassure her,
she in her apron,
dusted with icing and flour,
and he too self-contained, too rudely male,
more awkward, now, than when he knew her first:
a marriage come between them, all those years
of good intent
and blithe misunderstanding.
It was Tom Dow who brought her home,
tears in his eyes, the boy we had always known
as the local bully, suddenly finding himself
heroic,
and when they brought her in
and sat her down,
we gathered to stand
in the light of her, life and death
inscribed in the blue of her eyes, and the sweet
confusion of rescue, never having been
endangered.
She's married now, and Tom is married too,
and I, like my father, strayed into
discontent,
not being what was wanted, strange to myself
and wishing, all the time,
that I was lost,
out at the end of winter, turning away
to where the dark begins, far in the trees,
darkness and recent cold and the sense of another
far in the trees, where no one pretends
I belong.

He had been there since '55,
his lungs thick with smoke
and urea, the wicks of his eyes
damp, like the walls
of the furnace he tended for years,
till they laid him off.
He'd thought he would be glad
to say goodbye;
but that last shift, walking away
with the cold flask and rolled-up newspaper
tucked in his coat,
he turned to the sudden black
where the ovens had been:
wet slag, and frost on the tracks
and the last sacks of by-product
shipped out to beet-farms
and landfill.
With severance pay
and two years to go till his pension,
he had money enough
to survive;
but he hated to see himself
idle, a man on his own,
his wife dead, his grandchildren grown
and moved away.
He rarely saw his son;
though, once, in a bar
on the Beanfield, he found him
sitting alone with the *Mirror*:
Natalie Wood had drowned
in the ocean, near Catalina,
a hint of champagne
on her breath, and the longtime
child star's bewildered smile

a memory now, as she stared up
out of the picture
and both of them, father and son,
remembered how, long ago,
they had almost
loved her, miming that song about time
through her immigrant smile
that neither could disbelieve
as hard as he tried
– *somewhere, a time and a place* –
since there has to be something.

FIRST SIGNS OF AGEING

Being was never my forte; cold red wine
and glimmer of herd instinct bearing me into a night
that any fool could travel, if he chose.
I much prefer the moment's
absence, like the scent
of tulips in the hall and women calling
softly, from one landing to the next,
a moment since.
I never understand what they are saying,
but something they love
is retrieved from the huddle of knowing
again and again, the justice of should-have-been
in place of what never was.
I think of them now as sisters, as I think
each footfall is a mirror where I keep
the secret I never told, a childhood game
persisting on the cold side of away
and should-have-been a house
I know, the way a blind man knows the house
he lives in, blind from birth and every room
laid out for none to see, in steps and echoes.

DISCARD

Ma sarà troppo tardi; ed io me n'andrò zitto
tra gli uomini che non si voltano, col mio segreto.
                                                    Montale

I was out in the woods, picking mushrooms,
light in the higher boughs, a year-long
quiet in the shadows, spots of moss

and pea-gall — but nothing to keep:
Orange Peel, Fly Agaric, Dead Man's Eyes;
no ceps, the puffballs blown, the ground a drift

of beech leaves and broken twigs, my hands so cold
that, when my fingers brushed
the snakeskin, I imagined it alive: the child in me

awakened to the old
forebodings of his tribe.
It must have been discarded months before

yet, though it was paper-thin
and shapeless, there was still
pattern and colour enough to trouble me

with adder, hints of Braille, then sepia,
that made me think of you — I can't say why;
but walking home empty-handed, I half-believed

that nothing would be there, the house shrugged off
and a gap where the door should have been, where I'd suddenly
   learn
how long I have lived here alone, *col mio segreto*.

TRAVELLING SOUTH, SCOTLAND, AUGUST 2012

Necessity is not the mother of invention; play is.
Ian D. Suttie

It gets late early out here
in the lacklustre places,
wind in the trees and the foodstalls'
ricepaper lamplight, fading and blurred with rain,
the wire fence studded with fleece
and indelible traces
of polythene wrapping; marrowfat clogging the drains
on the road that runs out to the coast
then disappears.
A last bleed of gold in the west, like a Shan Shui painting,
then darkness.

The animals are gone
that hunted here:
wolves coming down from the hills, that
immaculate hunger,
rumours of bear and cat, quick
martens and raptors.
The rain is darker now,
though not so black,
oil-iridescent, streaked with the smell of lard
– *it gets late early out here*; though *late*, out here,
has a different meaning:

stars in the road
and the absence of something more
than birchwoods or song,
pallet fires, tyre-tracks,
grubbed fields clouded with grease
and palm oil, hints

of molasses and lanolin, tarpaper,
iron filings.
A narrow band of weather on the road,
then houses; though we scarcely think of them
as that.

I remember a meadow at dusk
in another rain
(and this is nostalgia now); I remember
I stood in a wind like gossamer and watched
three roe fawns and a doe
come quietly, one by one, through the silvering grasses,
wary, but curious, giving me just enough space
to feel safe,
their watchfulness reminding me of something
lost, a creaturely
awareness I could only glimpse

in passing.
That meadow is gone, and dusk
isn't dusk any more
– or not out here –
just miles of tract and lay-by on the way
to junkyards and dead allotments,
guard dogs on tether,
biomass, factory outlets,
the half-light of ersatz dairies petering out
on rotting fields
of rape and mustardseed.

We've been going at this for years:
a steady delete
of anything that tells us what we are, a long
distaste for the blood warmth and bloom
of the creaturely: local
fauna and words for colour, all the shapes

of ritual and lust
surrendered where they fell, beneath a fog
of smut and grime and counting-house
as church, the old gods

buried undead beneath the rural sprawl
that bears their names, or wandering the hills
of Lammermuir and Whitelee, waiting out
the rule of Mammon, till the land returns
– with or without us –
chainlink going down
to bindweed, drunken
thistles in a sway
of wind and goldfinch on the dead estates, fat
clusters of moss
and gentian, broken

tarmac with new shoots
of coltsfoot breaking through
like velvet, till the darkness of the leaf
unfurls into a light we could have known
but failed to see
by choosing not to find
the kingdom-at-hand:
this order;
this dialectic;
this mother of invention,
ceaseless play.

INSTRUCTIONS FOR A SKY BURIAL

Three miles west of Sue and Gerry's house
I found what remained of a young
coyote; how long dead, I couldn't say,
though all the soft tissue was gone, the eye-sockets
hollow, the viscera
scraped from the crib of the bone, leaving only the glare
of spine and a tatter of hide,
bald at the forelegs and black where the mouth had become
a rueful ventriloquist's grin.
It's hard to walk away from such a find;
there is something about a dead thing out in the open
that draws us in, a kind of gravity
both intimate and fateful, and I went back several times
to stand there, in the queasy sway of it,
flesh of its flesh, so it seemed, yet powerless
to wish it back to life
                    – though that was what I wanted: like a child,
I wanted to make it well, to resurrect
the light in its face, the attention, the changing colours.
I remember I used to come home through the ash
and graphite of the woods on Fitty Road,
the shadows mauve and grey between the trees
and subtle, always shifting, so it seemed
a presence in the land was out to play.
On days when I timed it right, I walked back
in the blue hour, when the stands
of thistle in full seed were incandescent
– no other word for it, everything lit with a pale,
cold flame.
                    I found a sheep there once, a slur
of lanolin and rot, the fleece
yellowed and bare in patches, one eye
more or less intact, a pool
of verdigris I didn't dare to touch,

though, up till then, I'd thought I was afraid
of nothing.
It shamed me for days, remembering how I'd lost
my nerve and run away,
guilty of something – though *what* I couldn't tell –
alone in the dark and suddenly wanting my mother.
They say the dead still listen for a time
before they leave for good, the spirit
sifting away in the wind, or salting the grass
for the life of the world to come.
Maybe it's this that decides
the new beginning, someone
coming across a field
at evening, birdsong
high in the trees, or the first dark spots
of rain in a stand of nettles: everything
shapes what it encounters, glancing touch
or intricate refusal, requiem,
or silence.
So when that day arrives
when I shall die,
carry me out of the house, unwashed and naked,
and leave me in the open, where the crows
can find me,
dogs, if there are dogs – there will be rats,
but let them eat their fill, so what they leave
can blend into the soil
more easily.
Some moisture will be lost
to heat and wind
but something more will live again
as fodder: meadow-grass
and daisies, rue
and hawthorn, all the living knots
of larvae in the scattering of flesh
and bone, birds gathering the hair

to line their nests, the last ants
busy about the mouth while something
inexact and perfect forms itself
around the last faint wisp
of vein, or tendon: something like a song,
but taking shape, implacably itself,
new breath and vision, gathered from the quiet.

Natural History

FIRST FOOTNOTE ON ZOOMORPHISM*

It seems we have said too little about
the heart, *per se*,

how it sits in its chambered nub
of grease and echo

listening for movement in the farthest
reed beds – any feathered thing will do,

love being interspecific, here,
more often than we imagine.

If anything, I'd liken us to certain
warblers, less appealing in the wild

than how we'd look
in coloured lithographs,

yet now and then, I'm on the point of hearing
bitterns at the far edge of the lake,

that cry across the marshes like the doom
you only get in books, where people die

so readily for love, each heart becomes
a species in itself, the sound it makes

distinctive, one more descant in the dark,
before it disappears into the marshes.

---

* 1. Attribution of animal form or nature to a deity or superhuman being. 2.
Imitation or representation of animal forms in decorative art or symbolism. (*The
Shorter Oxford English Dictionary*)

THE WISDOM OF INSECURITY

Not wanting to die was another universal constant, it seemed.
            J. Robert Oppenheimer

Place names are bleeding slowly from my mind
till nothing is left but

Uruguay – which someone told me once
means 'river of birds'

in the language of those who were killed
to make it ours.

I think of the symbols they made
on slices of doeskin or bark, when they went

upriver, as we all do when defeat
is casually dishonoured by the ones

who tricked us, flag-white egrets in the trees
flailing from branch to branch as the boat slides past,

but silent, like a person who has learned
to do without the self as worthy foe,

settling, instead, for something in the night
that tracks him from afar, some faint device

unspooling in an empty Nissen hut,
the data insufficient to predict

a future he could happily imagine,
no universal constant, no dark matter,

only a spill of cipher across the floor,
mile after mile of wavelength, feigning desire.

IN THE WOODS

I don't want to know about Keats
or Audubon,

though now and then a line from Clare sneaks in
and such fauna as I only half-imagine

are ghosts out of Bewick
or Catesby, rising softly through the fog,

the unrehearsed existence
of the backwoods, forms unseen

then glimpsed, before the swim
of vanishing.

It's something like a prayer, to be forbidden
perfect specimens, the finished articles

of lithogravure, field guides, Latin names
reducing everything

to *ruber*,
or *pubescens*.

A few yards further and the fog begins
to brighten, daylight bleeding through the trees

and a flicker of noise, or panic, off to the left,
where something should have been, and almost was.

EARTH

David 'Gypsy' Chain, killed while protesting the clearcutting of Californian Redwoods, Humboldt County, September 1998

Too late to say it aloud, but what I love
are phantom birds and girls with parasols

in paintings that no one looks at any more, the breathless
quiet of *pentimenti* sealed in the pigment;

and every living thing that went extinct
before a man could name it, unknown

hummingbirds and tree frogs, fig-trees, orchids,
aeons of filmy fern gone down to coal, lost

redwoods veined with centuries of light
and the faint but indelible stain of a living man

who died because he trusted to the earth
the heart he had kept intact, though no one in these parts

speaks any longer of hearts, or the sound in the trees
that once was a spirit and now is no more than the wind.

A FROST FAIR

That old cliché: it seemed that time
had stopped;

and people we thought we knew
came quietly out of the cold

to meet us.
Some people said

it had something to do with the sun,
and some, with how the planets were aligned,

but when the river froze
we walked into an air

we'd never breathed till then, our strange companions
smiling, as we pitched our tents and stalls,

happy to see the flags
and bunting, as if yellow was a thing

they'd never seen before – and red, and green –
as if, for them,

the world was always white:
snow on their lips and hands and a shine in their eyes

that made us think of children like ourselves
watching a magic lantern in the dark

and falling, through slide after slide,
into understanding.

STICKLEBACKS

If only something else had been so real
we might have left them in the Fitty Burn,
the males electric blue
and crimson, females
silver in the flank
and wall-eyed,
when they slithered through our fingers;

but summers were always for hunting, a garland of bees
trapped in a Kilner jar, the hum of it
gorgeous to the hand, all life and rage
made abstract; redpolls
lured into a homemade
box-trap for my cousin's backyard
aviary, their throats and crowns

the rose-red of the Zephirine Drouhin
in our grandmother's pit-town garden
at Crosshill.
When fair days came, we stood
like herons, knee deep in the silt
and slither of the rockpools, dip-nets
poised to gather in the shining wisps

of wrasse and weever, distant, nameless lives
that paled to nothing
in the noonday sun,
just as the lunties died in their chicken-wire frames
and the sticklebacks dimmed in their jars till we grew dismayed
and would surely have given them back
if we'd only known how,

come to a stop in an acre
of willow herb, dusk on the way
and the colours of everything, grassweed and Himalayan
balsam, butterflies
and lily beetles failing in the grey
that came to find us, calling us by name,
anchor and limit, singling us out for the dark.

PEREGRINES

Soon they will kill the falcons that breed in the quarry
(it's only a matter of time: raptors need space
and, in these parts, space equals money);

but now, for a season, they fly low over the fields
and the thin paths that run to the woods
at Gillingshill,

the children calling out on Sunday walks
to stop and look
                        and all of us
pausing to turn in our tracks while the mortgaged land

falls silent for miles around, the village below us
empty and grey as the vault where its money sleeps,
and the moment so close to sweet, while we stand and wait

for the flicker of sky in our bones
that is almost flight.

ALCOOLS

I *poison doux et chaste*

The true griefs are eager as mink
and nothing consoles them,

no catalogue of mothering or sails,
no time and tide, no token of repentance.

Out in the yard,
at the near edge of mudslick and rain,

your skin wastes away
in its birdcage of milksop and rubble,

that stain where the mouth should be
like unravelled yarn,

a *cri de coeur*, a toast,
a false confession,

your life as a hymn tune,
strung out on fishhooks, like worms.

II *noble et tragique*

It's never the tragic and noble
you like to imagine,

this minor key of having been bereft
for years, before you chance upon a field
of mud and thistles in the summer rain

and see it clear: the weather of a heart
so commonplace, you think it must belong

to someone else.
There's nothing sweet and chaste: the actual poison
spreading in your blood is just a mix

of chalk and sugar, grains of powder-blue
and rose-red, while the life that was to come

is something on the wind, until the wind
decays along a wire of thorns and gravel.

III *Passons passons puisque tout passe*

I found a goldfinch
injured in the grass

and carried it into the house
for a moment's shelter.

It didn't live
and that was no surprise

but even as it faded
from the light

I felt its mercy,
something only half-

imagined, and more gift
than I can say,

grace being such a thing
as I find small

too readily, distracted from the light
of what there is

by what I thought
I wanted.

IV *le bruit parmi le vent*

They say there are children, still,
in the furthest meadows.

In hollows of chalk and moon
they make their beds

from Lady's-smock
and strands of Old Man's Beard;

like pilgrims turned away
from blessèd knucklebones

or locks of hair,
they have that look

of having come too far
to be forgiven.

Beguiled by their *vita nuova*,
I love them well

and bait my snares for them
on warm nights, when the wind is like a veil

between the apple orchard
and the field;

and they have come
to love me well enough

to stay clear of my traps
till morning,

when I go out at first light
and gather up the shadows they have left

like hints of pike
and wolfskin in the grass,

wisps of the new life
snagged between trigger and spear.

SELF PORTRAIT AS AMNESIAC

I never saw the fauna of this world,
only a stare through headlights, a hurried

lurching from verge to verge
on a woodland road;

and, long ago, those places in the roof
where dust had gathered,

shoeboxes lined with eggs and empty
pomegranates drying in a bowl,

mousebones and wicker, chess pieces, muddy coats,
the slender, puppet versions of myself

who played here for a while
then moved away.

At times, when I have nothing else to do,
I think of going up into the highest

roof-beam, like the bridegroom in a hymn,
and bringing something down, an ancient

bird mask, or a broken violin,
or something in a cage that's still alive

until I fetch it out into the light
and watch it go to powder, teeth and eyestitch

crumbling, and the sound it used to make
extinguished, like the shrieking in the woods

that, once, when I was small, and still awake,
uncharmed me from my bed, before it vanished.

NOCTURNE: CHRISTMAS, 2012

a late quartet, a parting song
bequeathed by the great dead in perpetuity.
Dennis O'Driscoll

When I heard you had died, I went out into the yard
and stood a while, like something that belonged
to darkness: stars, a hard wind from the east,
a scent I couldn't place along the hedge
and, as I listened, weary of the gleam
from down below, the village like a shipwrecked
ferry, gardens strung with coloured bulbs,
forecourts and decking silver in the dark,
I heard a thin, far loophole in the wind
that sounded like a voice.
Nothing to do with you, I'm sure of that,
it would have been some animal event,
a low moan under the roof of my neighbour's barn
that might have been desire, or passing grief,
or further uphill, in a riddle of steel and fleece
the panic of some trapped, defenceless thing.
We all need a second life, the one we have
goes spinning away too soon, so we barely see
the flowers at our feet, the northern sky,
the otters and sunbirds straggling towards extinction
while, lodged inside the covers of our books
their images persist, immaculate
in photolithograph.
Say what you will, all making is nostalgia,
hurrying back to name the things we missed
the first time, when the world seemed commonplace:
a pail of water, standing by the hearth,
little owls hunting in pairs along a hedge,
a late quartet, a waltz, a woman singing,

that Christmas Eve, far in the hills, on a country road,
when the headlamps snagged on a ewe, in the first wet snow
and I stopped, by the side of the road,
to untangle the wire.

EROSION

For the wind passeth over it, and it is gone;
and the place thereof shall know it no more.
                                                    Psalm 103

Alone at home,
I'm working in the yard,
sun-warmed, a breeze off the coast,
the farmer from over the road
laying waste to his fields,
loam gone to dust in the heat; I can see it
gusting away.
He's lived like this for years, friendless and hard
in the artery, heart silting up,
a cloud in his eyes
from the effort of grim calculation.
His horoscope is rain and subsidy
and little else.
I keep myself busy. The native
birdlife calls from the stones
and hedgerows, chiffchaff
and starling, dunnock, the elegant
wren by the wall and the usual
flash mob of crows at the gate, all flutter and strut,
where something has died
in the wheels of a passing car
— *Bless the Lord, O my soul, and forget not all*
his benefits —
I remember my grandfather
reading his sun-paled
Psalter, his arthritic fingers
pitted with coal-dust and age, the first bloom of cancer
sweeter than new-mown hay
through the lingering smell

of whisky
and Oxydol
– *As for man, his days are as grass;*
as a flower of the field, so he
flourisheth – thistle
and mayweed, ground elder, Yorkshire Fog,
the sap on my hands drying fast
in the afternoon heat,
the thistledown drifting away
to another season
and part of me gone
in its wake, a wind-slender
kinship of sea and blood
and the kinship of earth
with everything that crawls beneath the stars
– *For he knoweth our frame; he*
remembereth that we are dust.
Half a mile down the hill, my neighbour is turning
his quad bike in circles, the panicked sheep bounding away,
the grass scorched and dead
in his tracks, the fences scabbed
with polypropylene
and muddled wool.
Soon he'll have turbines up; soon he'll buy out
my better neighbours, building, field by field,
his proud catastrophe
of tin and mud.
I loathe him, but it's nothing personal;
he's only one of many, motiveless
and carefully indifferent to all
he cannot buy or use, a friend
to no one, and yet not enough in him
of worth or life
to qualify as foe.
The birds fall still. The sky begins to cloud.
Far in the distance,

a pleasure boat
stalls on the firth.
I put away my tools and go inside:
it's silent for a moment, calm
and quiet, with a sense
of something interrupted, life
and conversation running in the land
in spite of us, who are no more to it
than chatter, or a species
of erosion.

YAWP

I sound my barbaric YAWP over the roofs of the world
                                    Walt Whitman

It wasn't the sound I wanted, or the thing
I hoped for, when I went into the woods

– nine years old and ready to be safe
elsewhere.

I wanted charms and songs. I hoped for
tiny bodies gathered from the dew

and folded in a length
of muslin, bruiseless surrogates of bone

and feather I could stitch into their cells
with scarlet cotton, singing them to sleep

or setting them, like candles, in a crib
of thorn and elder, ready for the first

good snow.
I never even thought of resurrection;

though now and then, grown old,
and safe no more,

I feel that needle working in its slub
of fabric, and the inference of matter

beating at my hand, more animal than faint
unravel, come to life beneath the skin

and tapping, softly, for the first drawn breath,
a muss of down, a beak, a nub of wing.

CHOIR

I think, if I tried, I could go back and sing again
no worse than I did at twelve, when my voice broke too soon
and I moved to the back of the choir on practice days,
mouthing the words and hoping that no one would hear
the missing soprano.
I stayed for the sudden dark at the stained glass window,
the sense of a vigil it gave me, like waiting for snow
at the presbytery door, a shape stealing in from the cold
to claim me for some lost kingdom; I stayed for the candles
and, off to the side of the altar, the theatre of absence
that made more sense, to me,
than our Sunday School God.

Close to retirement, the choirmaster hammered away
at the upright piano,
not for a moment
deceived, so much
in tune with us, he knew each voice by name,
the way a herdsman knows his animals:
the Cunningham twins, their faces so alike
that no one could tell them apart, until they sang;
the Polish boy, Marek; the grammar school beauty who smelled
like cinnamon after the rain
– he knew us all by heart, each voice he heard
combining with every child he had taught to sing
through a lifetime of choir, so thoroughly rehearsed
he swore he would pick us out
on Judgement Day.

I turned up every week for six months more;
and all that time he kept
my secret, each of us
pretending not to know the other knew.
I mouthed the words; he played; nobody guessed,

or everyone did; it doesn't matter now.
Later I switched to blues and The Rolling Stones,
Mandies and cider, Benzedrine, Lebanese;
so, though I wanted to, I couldn't
make it to Our Lady's on the day
they buried him next to his wife, in the steeltown rain,
to prepare for the Second Coming; and anyway,
despite the years of Kyries and hymns,
I never quite saw the point
of the life to come; back then it seemed
that, like as not, most everything runs on
as choir: all one; the living and the dead:
first catch, then canon; fugal; *all one breath*.

ACKNOWLEDGEMENTS

Acknowledgements are due to the editors of the following publications:

London Review of Books, New Statesman, Poetry Review, The Times Literary Supplement

'Tommy McGhee, Corby Works, 1981' was first published in *Jubilee Lines, 60 Poets for 60 Years*, edited by Carol Ann Duffy and published by Faber and Faber.

I would very much like to acknowledge the support of the Literarisches Colloquium Berlin for offering me the time and quiet to work on this book.